The Ever Conscious Crystal

By

Michael X Christopher

Thank you so much for purchasing this little book! My hope is that it will be a treasure for you, opening and expanding your mind to the endless possibilities contained within you.

Thank you to my family, friends, and everyone I have met along my path. I wouldn't be here without you.

Special thanks to Alexandra Fredricks, Bruce Todd, and Christina Migioia for their help in the creation of this story.

Michael X Christopher

Lion Lamb Legacy

This book was created by **Lion Lamb Legacy**, a collective of artists striving for a singular vision of worldwide peace, love, and respect for all creation. Check out our other titles and get involved at www.lionlamblegacy.com .

The Ever Conscious Crystal

My eyes opened in a flash. Surrounding me was my dimly lit one room apartment, overlooking the Delaware River. I couldn't believe I had the same dream again. I stumbled out of my clumsy twin bed, turning the television on with the remote control from my nightstand.

And now, for our featured story of the morning. For the fourth night in a row, millions of individuals across the country and around the world have reported having a very similar dream. In all instances, the individual found themselves in pursuit of a mysterious crystal. A crystal with the power to make their deepest desires manifest in the physical world. Some individuals are now in pursuit of that crystal, believing it actually exists. We spoke with Dante, a man on the hunt for the mysterious crystal.

I put the remote back down on the table and turned away from the television. I couldn't make sense of it. Why were we all having the same dream? In the dream it all felt so real. There was an energy emanating from the crystal, a powerful vibration that I felt throughout my whole being. Could it really exist?

Last night the dream had been more detailed than ever before. I was in the mountains in pursuit of the crystal. There was a sign that read Joy Mountain.

I pulled out my smart phone and looked up the name of the mountain. Holy Cow, I thought.

It exists! And it's less than two hours away.

Was the crystal really there? If I had seen the sign, had millions of others? I scanned the room, my eyes falling on the coffee table that was stacked high with bills and past due notices. Could this stone really improve my financial situation? Would it help me to become the writer I wished to be?

I was an amateur writer struggling to publish my first novel, working at an independent book store fifty hours a week for minimum wage.

The energy this crystal emitted, it made me feel like I could do anything.

I made up my mind right then and there. I was going in search of the crystal. What did I have to lose? I was off the next two days anyway. I might as well try.

I gathered some belongings and threw them into a nap sack, not even taking the time to brush my teeth or wash my face.

Slinging my back pack around my shoulder, I soared down three flights of stairs, and out onto the cold concrete below. My car was just around the corner in a two level garage.

I scurried along the street, absorbed in the thoughts of my own mind, when I collided shoulder to shoulder with another man.

"Hey! Watch where you are going!" I shouted.

"Me!?" the short statured man in an oversized sweatshirt replied.

The man stepped closer towards me.

"Oh, you got me at just the right time my friend. I'm hungry, and I need something to eat. Give me your wallet. Now!" the man shouted, pulling out a small navy blue pocket knife.

A jolt of tension flooded my body.

Not today. No not today, I thought.

The man's pale eyes locked with mine as he opened his mouth to speak again. "I said, give me your wallet! Before I take something else from you."

My hands dove into my pocket, grabbing a pile of cash and credit cards held together by a brown rubber band.

"Some wallet punk." the man said, grabbing it and taking off down the street.

What a way to start my day, I thought. That was all the cash I had on me, and my credit cards. I didn't even have enough gas to get to Joy Mountain now.

"Man!" I exclaimed. My eye catching a person slumped against the brick wall directly across the street.

"Did you see that?" I shouted. "I just got robbed."

The man against the wall had a card board sign in his hand that read, Free Inspirational Quotes.

It was nice to see a homeless person actively working for donations, instead of just begging.

"I saw everything." the man said.

He was dark skinned, in his mid-thirties, bald, and wearing blue jeans with a black jacket.

"I have no money." I said. "What am I going to do now?"

The man closed his eyes for a moment, too long for it to be a blink.

"You are searching for the Conscious Crystal, are you not?"

"Yes." I shuffled my feet in nervousness. "How did you know?"

"Never mind that. Listen, there is something you must know."

The man paused again, as if downloading the information from an external hard drive.

"There are two types of people in this world. There are those who put their trust in money, and those who put their trust in the Divine Mind. You are being forced to choose a side."

Just as he had finished speaking, the longest stretch limo I had ever seen pulled up. It was pure white, shining in exquisite extravagance.

A man decadently dressed in a grey pin striped suit exited the vehicle and began to walk toward us.

I looked over to my new found friend. He had a twinkle in his eye. An idea was forming in his mind. I watched as he opened his mouth to speak. "Excuse me sir. Do you have a moment? I would like to read you an inspirational quote to help you along your way."

"Get lost kid." the man said, straightening his suit jacket and brushing right past us.

The homeless man looked at me. "That, is someone who places his trust in money, disregarding the divinity and his fellow man."

"What were you going to tell him?" I asked.

"It was for him, and not for you. Now he will never know, but neither will you."

Ouch, I thought. That stung a bit.

"But, I don't understand. People need money to buy things. Like, I don't have money to buy gas for my trip in search of the crystal. Without money, how will I get there?"

"There are many ways. One must just be open to the possibilities and believe that the Magnificent One will provide the way." the man said, reaching into his pocket and pulling out a wad of cash.

"Where did you get all that from? How could you have so much money? You are homeless."

"Who said I was homeless? That is something you contrived in your mind based on my physical appearance and the fact that I carry a cardboard sign. Beware of the labels you place in your mind. I do this in my free time. At night I am a bellman at the FranklinVille Hotel."

"What the?" I started to say.

"Listen, perhaps I can help you out." the man said, as he leafed through his cash. "Here is twenty bucks."

"Thank you so much!" I said, "But twenty bucks will barely get me there. Let alone get me back. Do you think you could spare a little more?"

The man laughed out loud. "Who have you placed your trust in my friend? Money, or the Divine Mind?"

Chills coursed through my whole body. Oh man! I had chosen money, and so quickly.

The man realized my insight.

"Don't be so hard on yourself, friend. Just receive the $20 and be on your way. Give thanks and praise."

"Thank you." I exclaimed, to him and to anyone who could hear, to everyone and to no one in particular.

To the whole universe! "What is your name?" I asked, before turning to walk away.

"Emmanuel." the man said.

"It's nice to meet you Emmanuel. My name is Avery."

I inserted the key into my car, taking off out of the garage and onto the street. I put the destination into my GPS and began to let my thoughts drift mindlessly. This is crazy, I thought. Could I really find this crystal? And was it even real? I mean, it was probably just a dream. I should turn back, I thought. I could use the twenty bucks to buy breakfast and a coffee at the Cosmic Café.

No, I thought. I was going. I thought about what Emmanuel had said, about relying on money or the Divine. I had to put my trust in something. Why not the entire Universe?

I drove like this for hours, totally absorbed in the thoughts of my own mind. Before I knew it, city streets had turned to strolling mountainside bluffs. I was surrounded by steep turns and rolling hills. I eased my foot off the gas pedal, sliding down to 45 miles per hour. I was just driving along, enjoying the sites, when I sped past what appeared to be an elderly woman walking on the side of the road.

How bizarre, I thought. What was she doing walking by the road like that? Before I knew it, I had already passed her.

The last exit had been miles down the road, and who knew how far until the next exit? I felt an impulse inside. Something told me to stop. What if this woman needed help?

I pulled the car over to the side of the road and got out of the car, walking in the woman's direction. We were headed directly toward each other.

"Hello!" the woman exclaimed.

"Hi!" I said, "Are you alright?"

"Why yes! Of course! Just taking my morning stroll. Are you?"

"Me?" I asked. "Yes, I am quite fine. I was just…"

"Just worried about me? How thoughtful! Why thank you!"

Confused, I asked, "Aren't you scared, walking on the side of the road like that?"

The woman smiled, her wrinkled face lighting up in a youthful vibrancy.

"Afraid? Why no, of course not. I only meet wonderful people, people much like yourself."

I don't know if I am so wonderful, I thought.

"You see." the woman said. "The world is a mirror. It reflects back to you your thoughts and feelings. The world is a mirror in which we see ourselves." She paused for a moment, looking at me. "So, what brings a city kid like you out into the country?" the woman asked.

"What the, how do you know I'm from the city?" I asked, thinking the woman could read my mind.

"The way you're dressed." she replied. "Easy to spot a city boy."

"Oh." I said. I looked down at my khaki pants and blue button down shirt. I guess I did look like a city kid.

"Well you see, I am in search of a crystal. I believe it's in the mountains up that way."

The woman nodded. "Ah yes, I see. You are in pursuit of the crystal. Yes. I understand now."

The woman paused.

"Understand this. Everything you seek outside yourself you already contain within. Seek within to find that which is without. Do you understand?"

I nodded my head yes, but inside I felt, no. I did not know what she was saying.

The woman cocked her head ever so slightly to the side.

"Go." she said. "Peace and Love. Be well."

Immediately I turned to leave. I knew not to argue.

I could feel the command when she said, "Go". It was time to leave.

"Thank you." I said, still pondering the words she had said.

I walked all the way to my car, inserting the key into the door, and stepped inside.

Once in my car I looked through the rearview mirror. She was gone.

Just down the road I began to see signs for Joy Mountain. Joy Mountain 10 miles. Then 8 miles. Then 5 miles.

Less than one mile from the mountain my car began to sputter. I looked at the fuel indicator. Bright red. I had been on empty, and had not even known it. Up the road and immediately to my right I spotted a pull off. I eased the car into a dirt filled lot along the side of the road. I shifted the car into park as the engine went silent. Well, I thought, I guess I'm here.

The lot was empty except for two other cars. Were they too in search of the crystal?

I grabbed my nap sack and stepped out of the car.

There was a blue porta-potty directly to my right.

Thank you, Universe, I thought. All of that driving and I hadn't even stopped to go to the bathroom once.

I opened the door to the porta-potty and relieved myself. Once finished, I swung the blue door open.

What I saw stunned and mystified me.

The most beautiful girl I had ever seen. Dressed in a flowing brown and orange dress, that swayed in the wind like autumn leaves.

Speechless. I opened my mouth, but words could not be found.

"Hello." the girl said. "I am Sarah."

"I, I am Avery." I stuttered.

"It's such a beautiful day, isn't it? Can't you just feel the vibration of the trees? All of nature sings its song today." Sarah said.

"Uh, I uh. Yeah."

Sarah smiled. "Come with me." she said, extending her hand to me.

I clasped it, reluctantly. I mean, I wanted to hold her hand, but was this normal? Who held hands with a complete stranger? I was more worried for her, but I didn't know why.

We walked up the side of the road and turned right onto a tree lined trail that headed up the mountain. Yellow and orange leaves illuminated both the limbs of trees and the ground beneath our feet.

"Do you feel the peace and love that surrounds us?" Sarah said. "Nature is always at rest. Even amidst its ceaseless activity, there is harmony and peace. Can you see the harmony outside you? It is a direct reflection of the harmony within you."

"I am afraid I can't feel it. All I can feel are the ceaseless thoughts within my mind. Nervousness and tension surround me inside."

"Oh how I understand! I used to feel that way as well. Then I began to spend time in nature, in communion with life. Eventually, over time, I connected with the life inside of me. I realized that life, the life inside me, is the same life inside all things. The life inside of me is inside of you too. Here, let me show you."

Sarah pointed to a large flat rock on the side of the trail.

"Let's have a seat." she said.

"Now look around. Watch the leaves as they fall from the sky. See how they just let go. Observe the beauty as they fall. Witness their grace as they lie on the ground, dissolving into the dirt. Realize they are the nutrients for the soil that will nourish the season to come. Observe the life in what only appears to be death. Connect with it. Realize you are one with it."

I looked all around me. I watched as a leaf let go, dropping ever so softly into the dusty soil. My mind stilled, for just a moment.

"Now close your eyes. Realize this whole world is vibrating. Realize that it vibrates in harmony. Understand you are a part of that infinite harmony.

Recognize you are in harmony with all things, vibrating at the frequency of peace and love."

I closed my eyes. My mind was blank. For the first time I felt a bit of the stillness that lay inside. I imagined the whole world vibrating in harmony, singing a song of love and peace. I imagined it, and before I knew it, I was feeling it. To a degree, I was feeling it.

I opened my eyes in amazement, exclaiming, "Thank you!"

But when I opened my eyes, she was gone.

What the, I thought.

How did she? Where did she?

Suddenly I felt alone again. But the feeling I had felt was real. I had felt peace for the first time.

What to do now, I thought. I looked around me. All around me were silent shapes of orange and yellow. But what about the crystal?

I still hadn't found it, and now there was no way to get back. I was completely alone on a mountain I knew nothing about. I started to climb up the trail. It was a steady climb, with stones and branches scattered along the sturdy soil.

I peered through delicate tree limbs, in silent pursuit of what I had only seen in my dreams.

This was pointless, I thought. How am I going to find a stone, amongst thousands of stones, when I don't even know what I am looking for?

Suddenly, the foolishness of my decisions caught up with me. I was alone on a mountain. My car had run out of gas, and I had no idea what I was looking for, or if it even existed.

A wave of anxiety rushed over me.

Calm down, I thought. Think about the people you met. Think about Emmanuel, the woman on the road, Sarah. They were not coincidences. They couldn't be.

I was on the right path. I knew it. I just didn't know what I was looking for.

I climbed higher up the mountain. Hours passed. Early afternoon turned to images of evening. I climbed on.

I reached the summit as the sun was slowly fading behind neighboring peaks. Billowing clouds colored with streaks of magenta lofted through the sky.

The setting sun was both majestic in sight, and a symbol of fading hopes and dreams. It seemed I was wrong in coming to this mountain. Perhaps the crystal was, only in my dreams.

I turned my back to the setting sun and began to trudge back down the winding mountain trail. I was once again absorbed in the current of my own mind, until I stumbled across a tiny squirrel.

It had a nut in hand, and when it saw me it froze. I watched as it scurried up what appeared to be a giant oak. I stared, transfixed at the power of this mighty tree. Absorbed in its presence I felt compelled to sit beneath its gentle leaves.

I sat as the sky began to darken around me. Closing my eyes, I tried to meditate on the life that was inside. Remember what Sarah said, I thought.

The life that surrounds you is alive in you as well. I closed my eyes, feeling the vibration of the mighty tree. Is that the tree vibrating, or is it me?

I intensified my focus. Suddenly it seemed there was no distinction between the tree and me. A streak of light flashed across my mind's eye.

I opened my eyes in wonder. The light. A light was emanating from the darkness outside. Or was it a light from within? Either way. A bright light.

I climbed once again to the top of the mountain, determined to witness the source of this blinding, golden light.

As I came closer I became absorbed in a light bursting from the Peak of Joy Mountain. The light stretched straight upward to the heavens, illuminating the stars now strung across the expanse of night sky.

I stepped with both feet into the full presence of the light. My body pulsed with power of a thousand suns. **The Universe is Perfect Harmony,** I thought. Sounds of silent symphonies danced ever so gently in my mind. **The World is a Mirror.** I thought about the people I had met on my journey to Joy Mountain. They were instrumental in my getting here, without them there is no me. **I am the Crystal.** The crystal is inside me. Everything we seek without, we are to find within. **We are all One.**

www.ingramcontent.com/pod-product-compliance
Lightning Source LLC
Chambersburg PA
CBHW060607030426
42337CB00019B/3654